The Adventures of Maxine and Beanie
Maxine Goes to School!

"PAWS" JOURNAL

GOUDELOCK & THE 3 BEARS
PUBLISHING

Copyright ©2021 Goudelock and the 3 Bears Publishing
All Rights Reserved.

The Adventures of Maxine and Beanie: Goes to School was written by Karolyn Denson Landrieux and illustrated by Karen Light.

Spanish translations by Maru Caicoya
French translations by Pierre Landrieux

For resources and further inspiration, please visit us at:
maxineandbeanie.com and follow us on social media @maxineandbeanie

Printed in the United States of America

ISBN: 978-1-7377837-1-8

This journal belongs to :
Este cuaderno le pertenece a :
Ce journal appartient à :

_____

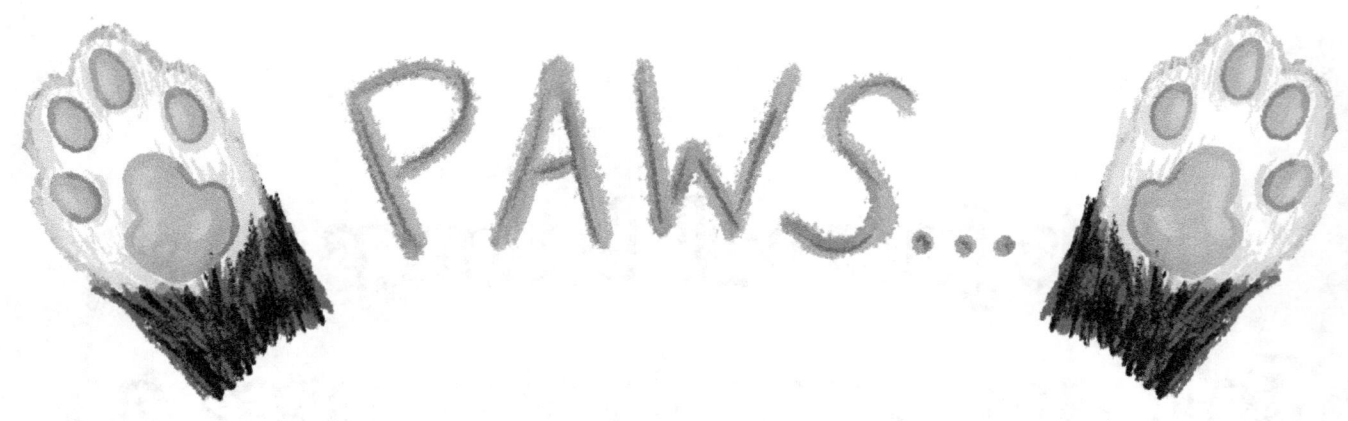

PAWS...

Do you like school? Why?
What is your favorite class?

¿Te gusta ir al colegio? ¿Por qué?
¿Cual es tu tarea favorita?

Aimes-tu l'école? Pourquoi?
Quelle est ta matière préférée?

PAWS...

Do you have a special outfit?
What makes you feel special when
you get to dress up?

¿Tienes un atuendo favorito?
¿Que te hace sentir especial cuando te
pones ropa bonita?

As-tu un habit special?
Qu'est-ce qui te fait sentir spécial
quand tu t'habilles?

PAWS...

What are important things to do when you are riding in a car that help to keep you safe? What games can you play on a long car trip?

¿Cuando viajas en coche, que es lo más importante para mantenerte seguro? ¿Que juegos puedes jugar en un largo viaje en coche?

Quelle est la chose importante à faire dans la voiture qui aide à rester en sécurité? A quels jeux peux-tu jouer pendant un long voyage en voiture?

15

PAWS...

What is something that you would take for show and tell? What makes it special? What is your favorite teacher's name?

¿Que te gusta llevar a mostrar y compartir? ¿Que lo hace espacial para ti? ¿Cual es el nombre de tu profesor favorito?

Qu'est-ce que tu aimerais apporter à l'école pour un exposé? Pourquoi est-ce spécial pour toi? Quel est le nom de ton instituteur ou institutrice préféré?

PAWS...

Do you have special best friends?
What are the names of some of your friends?

¿Tienes algún amigo especial?
¿Como se llaman tus mejores amigos?

As-tu des supers meilleurs amis?
Quels sont les noms de tes amis?

Thank you for going on adventures with us!

Gracias por ir de aventuras con nosotros!

Merci d'être parti en aventures avec nous!

www.ingramcontent.com/pod-product-compliance
Lightning Source LLC
Chambersburg PA
CBHW081423080526
44589CB00016B/2652